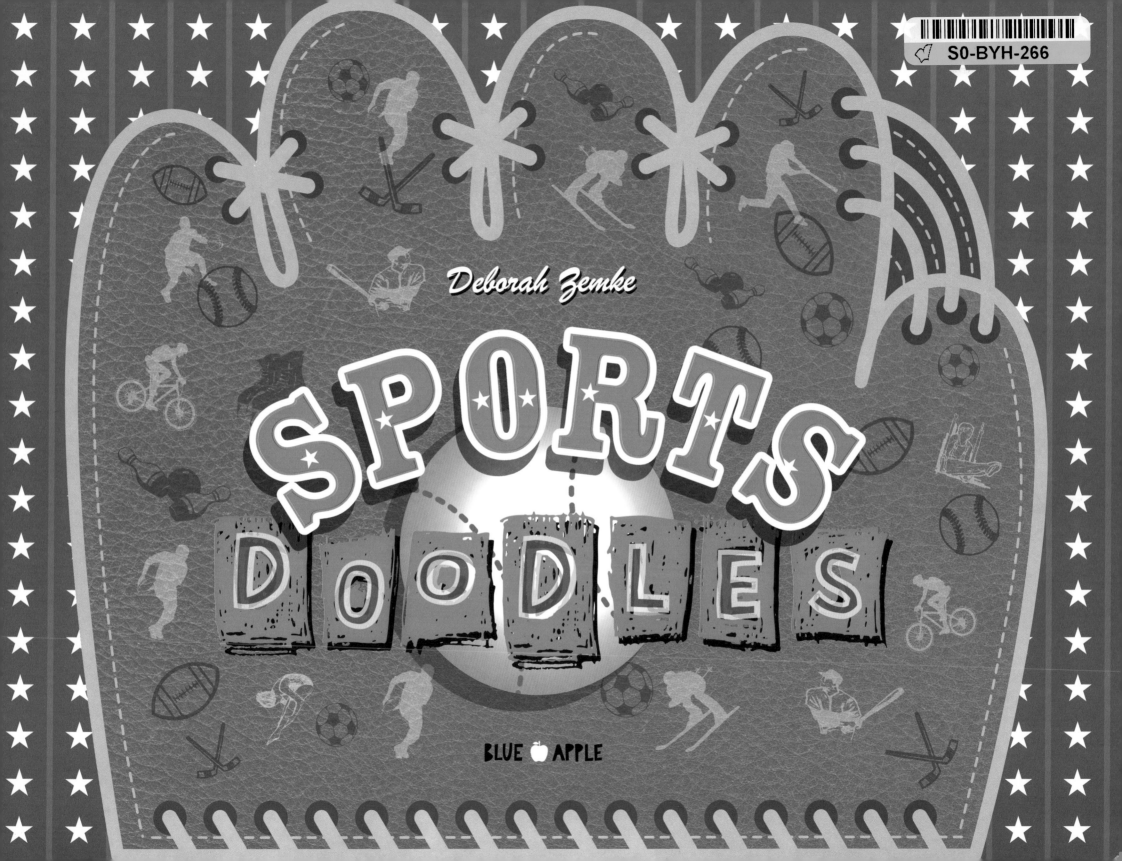

Deborah Zemke

SPORTS DOODLES

BLUE 🍎 APPLE

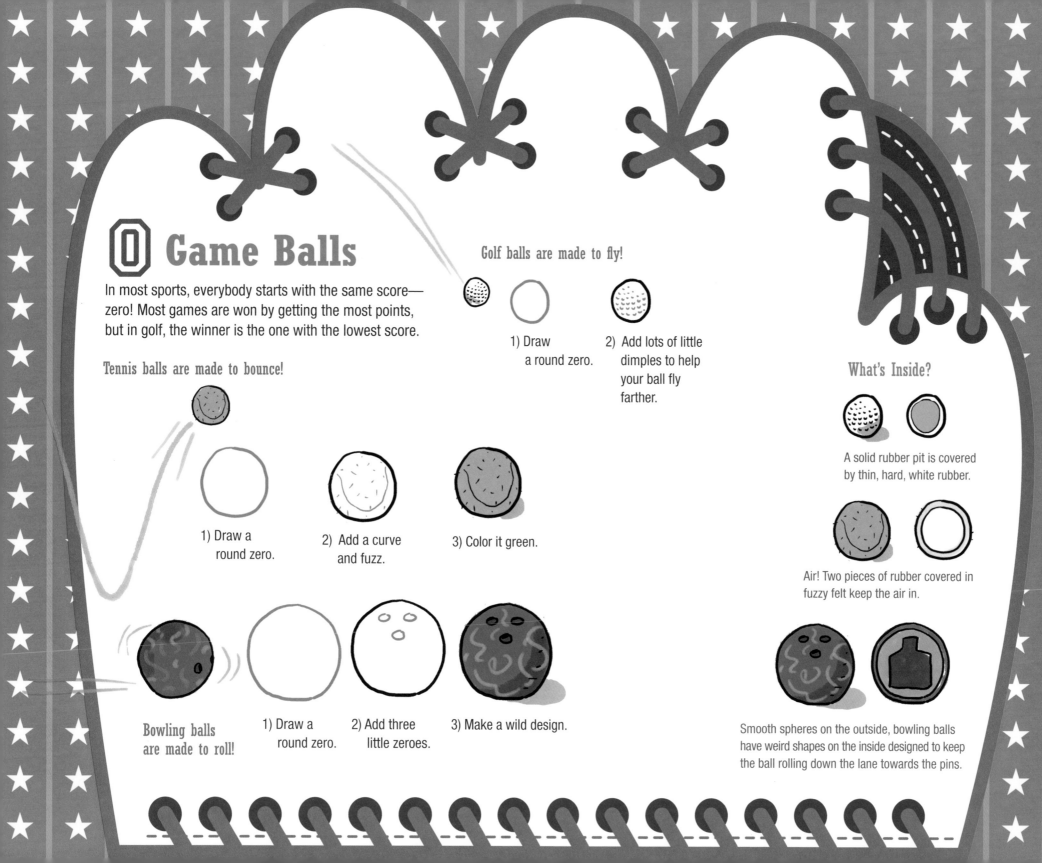

Game Balls

In most sports, everybody starts with the same score—zero! Most games are won by getting the most points, but in golf, the winner is the one with the lowest score.

Tennis balls are made to bounce!

1) Draw a round zero.

2) Add a curve and fuzz.

3) Color it green.

Bowling balls are made to roll!

1) Draw a round zero.

2) Add three little zeroes.

3) Make a wild design.

Golf balls are made to fly!

1) Draw a round zero.

2) Add lots of little dimples to help your ball fly farther.

What's Inside?

A solid rubber pit is covered by thin, hard, white rubber.

Air! Two pieces of rubber covered in fuzzy felt keep the air in.

Smooth spheres on the outside, bowling balls have weird shapes on the inside designed to keep the ball rolling down the lane towards the pins.

⓪ Fastball

Fire up your fastball to pitch a no-hitter! Or make it a perfect game with zero hits and zero walks. Hold the ball between your first and second fingers across the seam and your thumb on the bottom.

Here's what it looks like from the front.

How fast is a fastball? Some pros can throw a baseball close to 100 mph.

1) Draw a fat zero.

2) Add three waves . . .

3) a loopy thumb . . .

4) and a curved finger.

5) Add six curves . . .

6) and 56 red stitches.

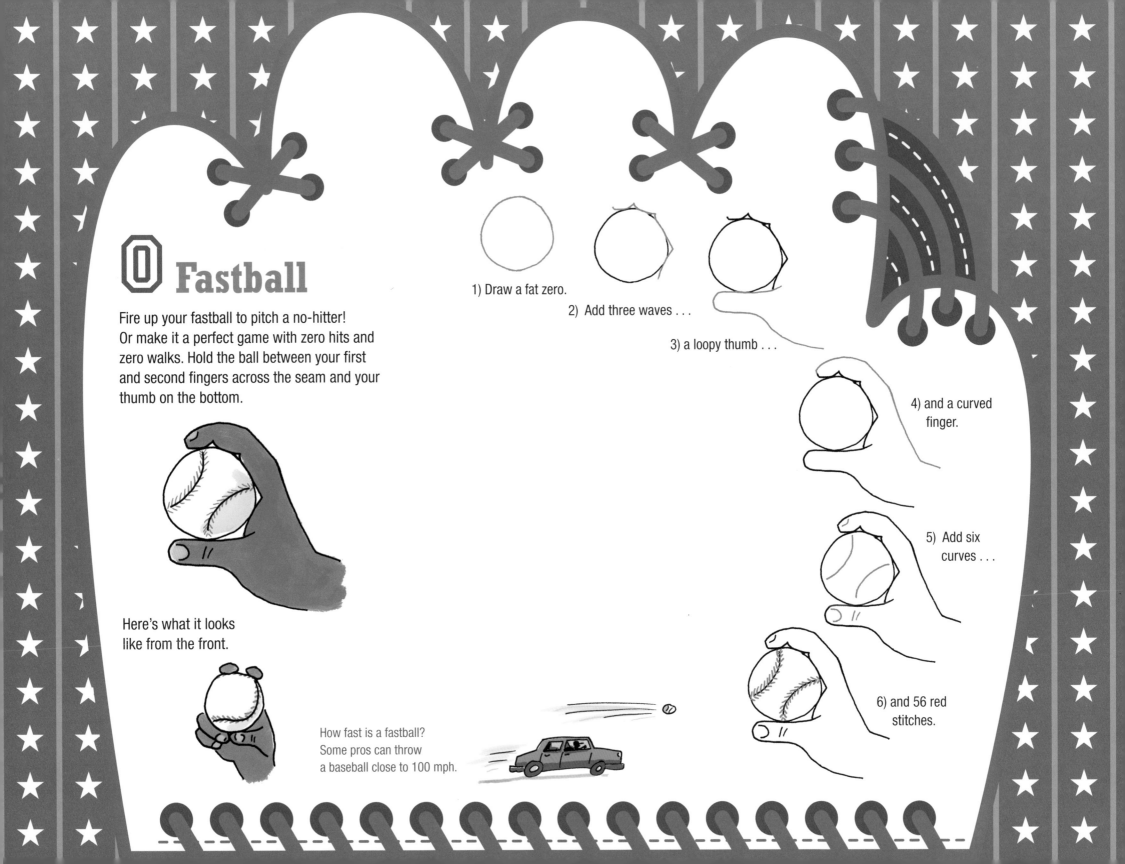

Ⓞ Tennis Racquet

Love means nothing when you play tennis! Nothing— as in zero! No one knows why zero is called love in tennis scoring, but it's certain that no one wins with love!

The score of this game is definitely love-love!

1) Draw a 0.

2) Attach a curvy V . . .

3) and a square U.

4) Add twelve lines across . . .

5) and ten lines down.

O Hockey Save

Saved! Say that 80 times—that's the most saves by a goalie in one game, made by Sam LoPresti, for the Chicago Blackhawks in 1941.

Goalies wear two different gloves: a rectangular blocking glove and a round catching glove.

1) Draw a zero.

2) Add a C . . .

3) and a V.

4) Attach two curves . . .

5) two more curves . . .

6) and a box.

7) Make criss-cross lines.

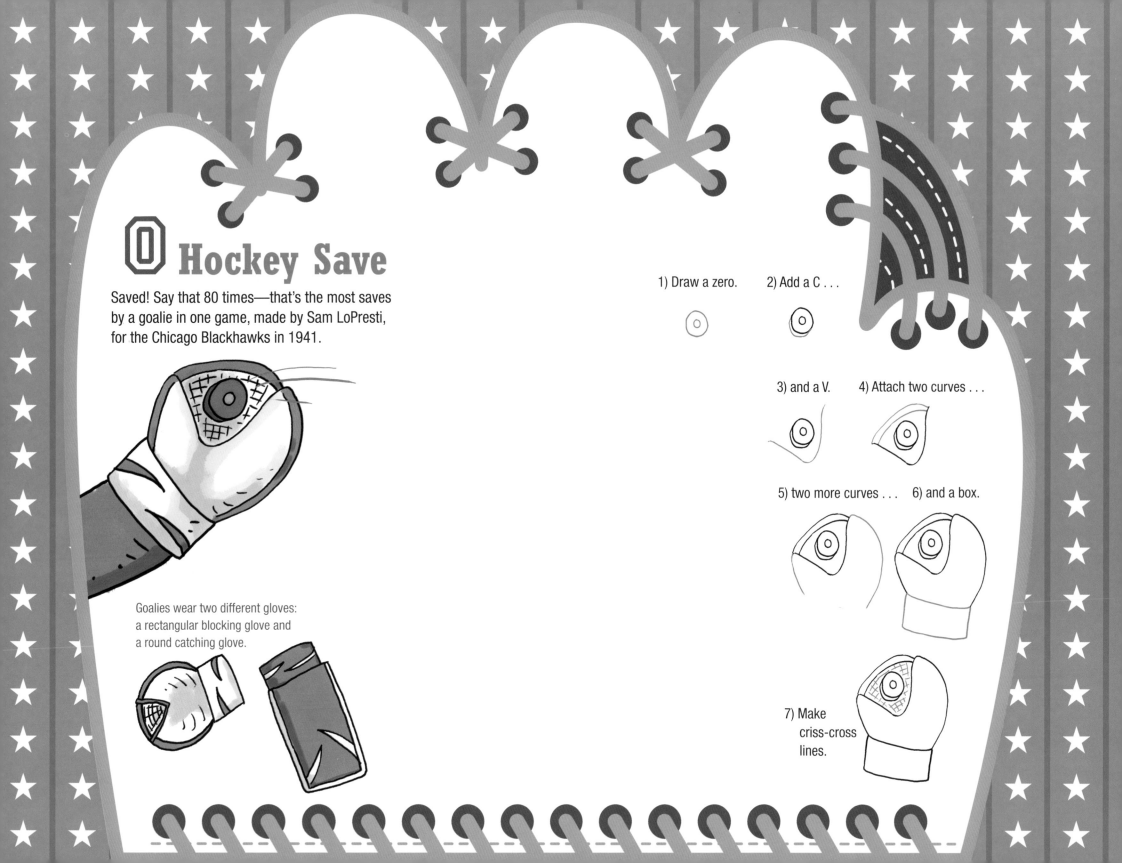

1 Golf Hole in One

It's a hole in one on Hole #1! In golf, you win when you get the lowest score.

Why didn't the golfer wear socks?

Because he had a hole in one.

1) Draw a skinny 1.

2) Add a sideways V.

3) Draw a small 1 in a circle.

4) Make a ring around the first 1.

5) Add a small circle . . .

6) and make it go!

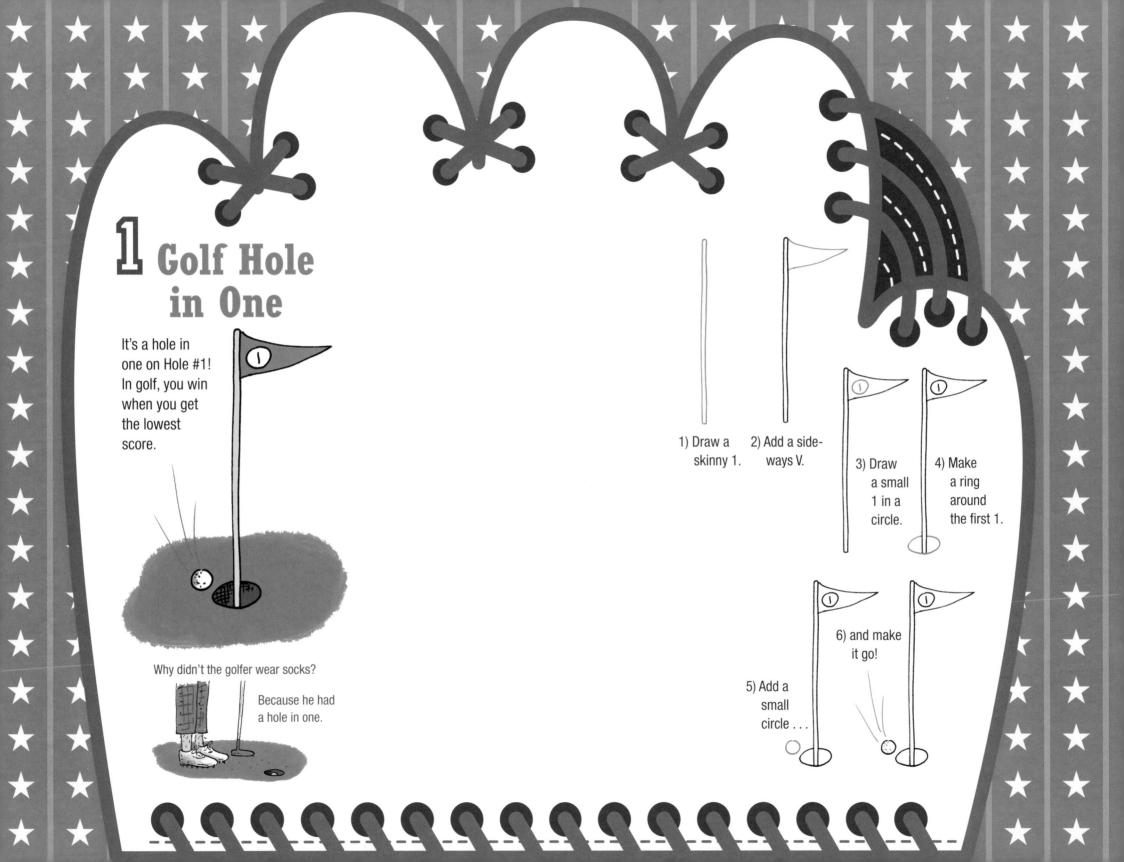

1 Tennis Serve

Whether you're playing cards or tennis, an ace is great! In tennis, an ace is when you serve and the other player doesn't even touch the ball.

Make a card for the Ace of Tennis.

1) Make a finger pointing 1 . . .

2) and a little 0.

3) Add three fingers and a wristband.

4) Make a sleeve and put your eye on the ball.

5) Add a sweatband and hair...

6) and put your hand on the racquet serving up an ace.

1 Baseball Bat

Crack!
That's the sound of
a wooden bat as it hits
the ball for a base hit.
Each bat is made of
1 piece of ash wood.

These are
some high-flying
baseball bats!

1) Draw a
slanted 1.

2) Attach
a long hook.

3) Draw four
loops one
way . . .

4) and four
loops the
other
way.

5) Add four
curves . . .

6) wood
grain . . .

7) and keep
your eye
on the ball!

1 Soccer Goal

Soccer is a game of 1's. There's 1 point per goal and 1 goalie per team of 11 players.

250 million players in over 200 countries make soccer the #1 most popular game in the world!

1) Draw two 1's. 2) Connect them at the top . . . 3) and attach two V's. 4) Connect the V's. 5) Draw vertical lines . . . 6) and horizontal lines.

2 Bicycle Race

Some bike races run in circles around a town, and others run thousands of miles across a continent. Some go up mountains, some across deserts. Whether a bike race is 10 miles or 1,000 miles, all are ridden on 2 wheels!

Draw a rider on this bike.

It's a mice-cycle built for two!

1) Add a 2 to the bike.

2) Make a leg and shoulder . . .

3) arm and chest.

4) Make a helmet...

5) and sunglasses...

6) bar and uniform.

2

Hockey Skate

Whizzing down the ice, gliding forwards, backwards, turning and stopping on a dime, hockey players skate as if their skates were part of their legs.

Here's a HAWKey player who can really fly down the ice!

1) Make a 2.

2) Add a curved L . . .

3) and eight loops.

4) Draw a big curvy L . . .

5) and an angled curl.

6) Draw another angled curl . . .

7) and make another skate.

The hoop is 2 times bigger than the basketball.

18"

9"

Look what would happen if the ball were 2 times bigger than the hoop!

2 Slam Dunk

Score a sure 2 points when you jump high and power the 9-inch diameter ball down through the 18-inch diameter hoop for a slam dunk!

1) Draw a curvy 2.

2) Make a loop . . .

3) and three more loops.

4) Add a big curve . . .

5) and four curves.

6) Jump up . . .

7) and stuff the ball in the net!

2 Skiing

Check out this **chimpan-ski** on the slopes!

Gravity powers this sport! Strap 2 pieces of wood to the bottom of your snow boots and fly down a mountain. You drive the ride with your 2 legs by turning across the slope.

1) Draw two 2's on the skis.

2) Add two curves . . .   3) and two more curves.   4) Draw two arms with mittens . . .   5) and a helmet. . .   6) and goggles.   7) Add poles and swoosh!

2 Baseball Glove

Who's ready to play a double header?

The shortstop fields the ground ball, steps on second base, pivots, and throws to first for a double play! They've turned 2 to end the inning!

1) Draw a 2.

2) Add four loops . . .

3) two curves across and seven criss-cross curves.

4) Make three curves . . .

5) three X's and thirteen pairs of small curves.

6) Catch the ball in the pocket!

Why did the frog play center field?

To catch flies!

2
Soccer Kick

2 feet are better than 1!
Soccer players
learn to kick well
with both feet so they
can control the ball
wherever they are on the field . . .
even when they need to kick the ball backwards!

1) Draw a 2.

2) Attach two curves.

3) Make shorts . . .

4) a Z leg . . .

5) t-shirt . . .

6) arms and head.

7) Put on your shoes, make a ball and kick!

3 Basketball Net

Swish! It's all net for 3! You score 3 points on a basket when you shoot further away from the basket, beyond the 3-point line.

Let's play some B-ball with a B-ball!

Careful! This Bee-ball stings!!

1) Draw a sideways 3.

2) Add two more.

3) Attach seven lines . . .

4) and six more lines.

5) Put a squashed O on top . . .

6) and shoot!

3

Hockey Hat-Trick

1) Add a 3 to the drawing.

2) Turn it into a glove.

3) Make another glove.

4) Connect them with a stick…

5) with a curved end.

6) Add a puck.

There's 3 for 3 in hockey! Hockey games are divided into 3 periods, and the rink is divided into 3 zones. When a player scores 3 goals in one game, it's called a hat-trick. But since players wear helmets, not hats, maybe it should be called a helmet-trick.

1 2 3

Make a uniform for your super shooter!

4 Football Helmet

Hut 2-3-4 hike! Football is a game of 4's. A team has 4 downs to move the ball 10 yards, and the game is divided into 4 quarters of 15 minutes each.

Make up a name for your own fantasy football team. Design a logo, either a picture or a letter, for your team's helmet. Here are some ideas:

Texas Flames

Detroit Power

Savannah Sharks   Nebraska Lightning

My football team is named

_____.

1) Draw a pointy 4.

2) Add another pointy 4.

3) Draw two lines . . .

4) and two V's.

5) Make a curve with a box on the end.

6) Draw a curve, a zero, and the logo of your fantasy team.

4 Baseball Grand Slam

This little bird is a home WREN!

Swing for the seats! If you hit a home run with the bases loaded, you score 4 runs with 1 swing of the bat!

The baseball infield is shaped like a diamond with a base at each of the 4 points.

1) Make a 4.

2) Add two lines.

3) Draw a helmet . . .

4) and shirt . . .

5) pants . . .

6) and shoes.

7) Draw an arm, bat, and swing!

4

Four Square

Four Square is fun math!
1 square divided into
4 squares plus
1 bouncing ball plus
4 friends equals fast fun!

Want to play? I got this foursquare ball for my birthday!

1) Draw a square 4.

2) Make Square 1 . . .

3) and Square 2 . . .

4) and Square 3 . . .

5) and Square 4.

6) Add a ball and friends.

5 Soccer Ball

It's a puzzle! Twelve 5-sided and twenty 6-sided flat pieces of leather fit together around a rubber balloon that's filled with air to make 1 round soccer ball.

5-sided
pentagonal shape

6-sided
hexagonal shape

5 goals are the most ever scored by one player in a World Cup match by Oleg Salenko in 1994.

1) Draw five lines shaped like a house in the center of the circle.

2) Add a line at one corner . . .

3) and four more lines at the other four corners.

4) Connect one line to the circle with a wide V.

5) Connect the other four lines to the circle.

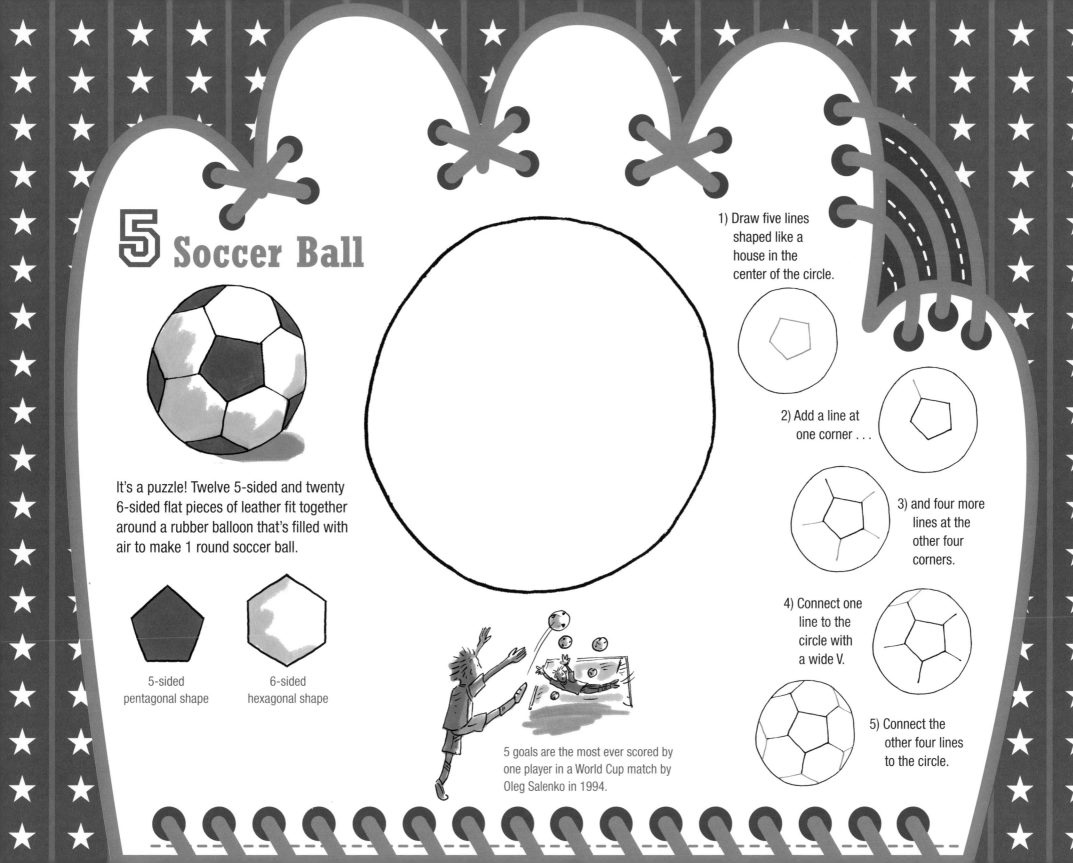

Why did the #1 guard wear a bib?

Because he dribbled a lot!

5

Basketball Team

There are five players on each team.

1 is the point guard,
2 is the shooting guard,
3 is the small forward,
4 is the power forward,
and 5 is the center.

1) Draw a 5.

2) Add two hands . . .

3) a face . . .

4) two arms . . .

5) jersey and shorts . . .

6) and legs and feet.

7) Add your favorite number and finish the uniform.

6 Surfing

It's all in the wave! People have been surfing for hundreds of years, catching reef break, beach break and point break waves!

Hang 10! That's surfing with all 10 toes hanging over the front of the board!

1) Add a funny face to the 6.

2) Draw two waving arms.

3) Add a belly and shorts . . .

4) two legs and feet.

5) Draw a surfboard.

6) Catch a 6-foot wave!

To catch a pass that's over your head, make a triangle with both hands, close your hands when the ball is halfway in, tuck the ball away, and run for the end zone!

6

Football Pass

The wide receiver is all alone in the end zone! He leaps in the air . . . he's got it! Touchdown! 6 points!

1) Draw a leaping 6.

2) Add two curves.

3) Make a helmet . . .

4) jersey and pants...

5) legs and feet.

6) Open your hands . . .

7) look up and catch the ball!

6 Volleyball

Take two teams of 6 players each, separate them with a net, toss in a ball, watch them hit, pass, set, jump, bump, spike, block, and dig!

Players "dig" a spiked ball by reaching it just before it hits the floor. No shovels are allowed!

1) Add three curves to the 6.

2) Draw two hands spread wide.

3) Make a sleeveless shirt . . .

4) shorts . . .

5) legs and feet.

6) Draw the net and uniform.

7
Hockey Stick

7 goals in one game! No pro player has scored more since Joe Malone did it in 1920—over 90 years ago.

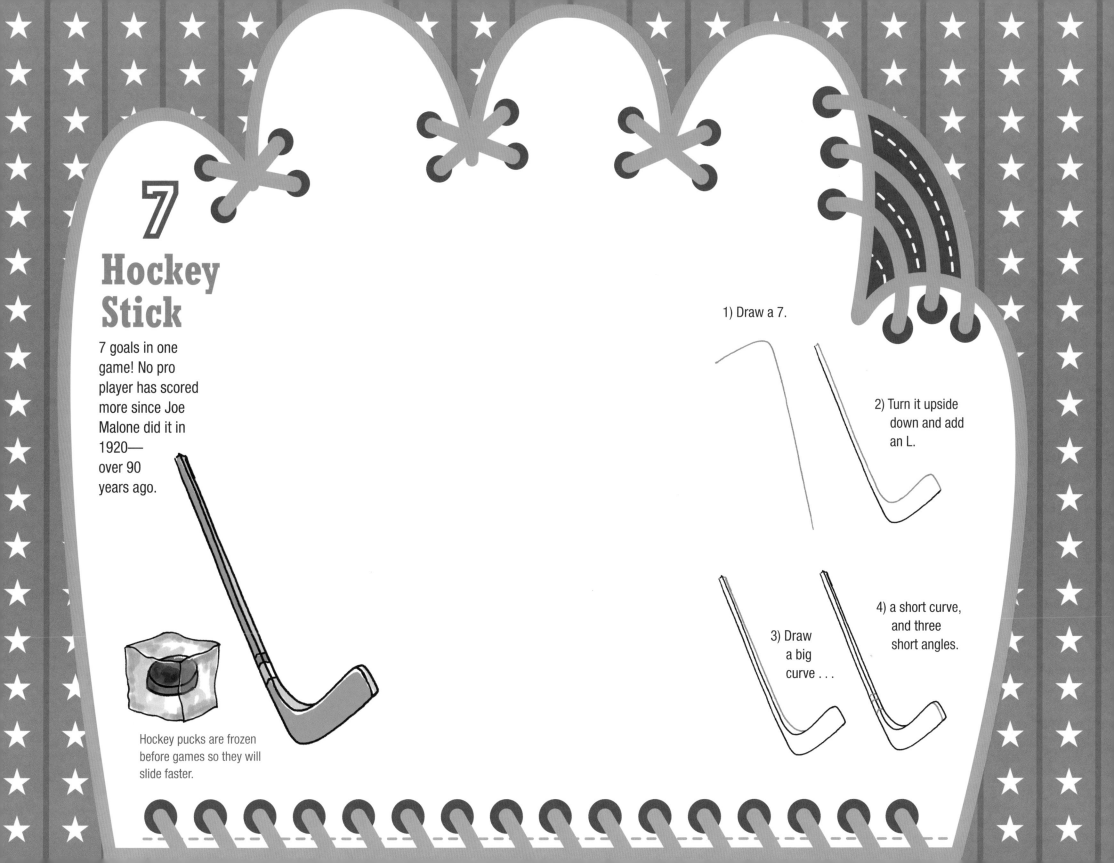

Hockey pucks are frozen before games so they will slide faster.

1) Draw a 7.

2) Turn it upside down and add an L.

3) Draw a big curve . . .

4) a short curve, and three short angles.

8 Ice Skating

Skate a figure 8—backwards! Figure skaters spin, jump, and glide across the ice. Speed skaters go in circles around the track as fast as they can—30 mph and more!

1) Add two 7's to the skate on the figure 8.

2) Draw another leg and skate.

3) Make a box with stars . . .

4) and two bent arms.

5) Draw a hat and scarf . . .

6) and smile as you glide.

Add another skater to the ice!

Have you ever seen mice skating?

9 Track

Quick as lightning, Usain Bolt is the world's fastest man. He ran 100 meters in 9.58 seconds.

The fastest man can run over 23 miles per hour, but that's way slower than these champs:

#1 cheetah—70 mph
#2 pronghorn—61 mph
#3 lion—50 mph

1) Attach a bent leg loop to the 9.

2) Add a straight leg loop.

3) Make shoes and shorts . . .

4) and shirt.

5) Draw two curves and a C.

6) Draw a U and two curves.

7) Make hands and head.

9 Baseball Catcher

9 players on each side play for 9 innings in pro ball. The catcher is the busiest player on the field.

9 9

Let's play baseBULL!

1) Add two hook curves to the 9's.

2) Draw two U's.

3) Draw a glove . . .

4) and mask.

5) Make three curves on each side . . .

6) and four more in the middle.

The 10 pins are set up to make a triangle.

7 8 9 10
4 5 6
2 3
1

1) Turn the 1 into one pin.

2) Draw another pin . . .

3) 3 and 4 pins.

4) Draw 5, 6, 7 pins . . .

5) 8, 9, and 10 pins.

6) Draw red stripes and throw a strike!

10 Bowling Strike

A bowling game has 10 frames, and you get 2 throws per frame. Knock all 10 pins down on your first throw and you score a strike for 10 points PLUS however many pins you knock down on your next 2 throws!

10 Gymnastics

Gymnasts start with a score of 10 and then get points subtracted for mistakes and added for difficulty. How difficult? Try doing a handstand 9 feet in the air without moving the rings!

1) Add a curve to the hands.

2) Draw two more curves.

3) Draw three more curves.

4) Add three more curves.

5) Draw loopy feet and a circle.

6) Make an upside down face.

7) Write a score for each of these judges. Who will give your gymnast a 10?

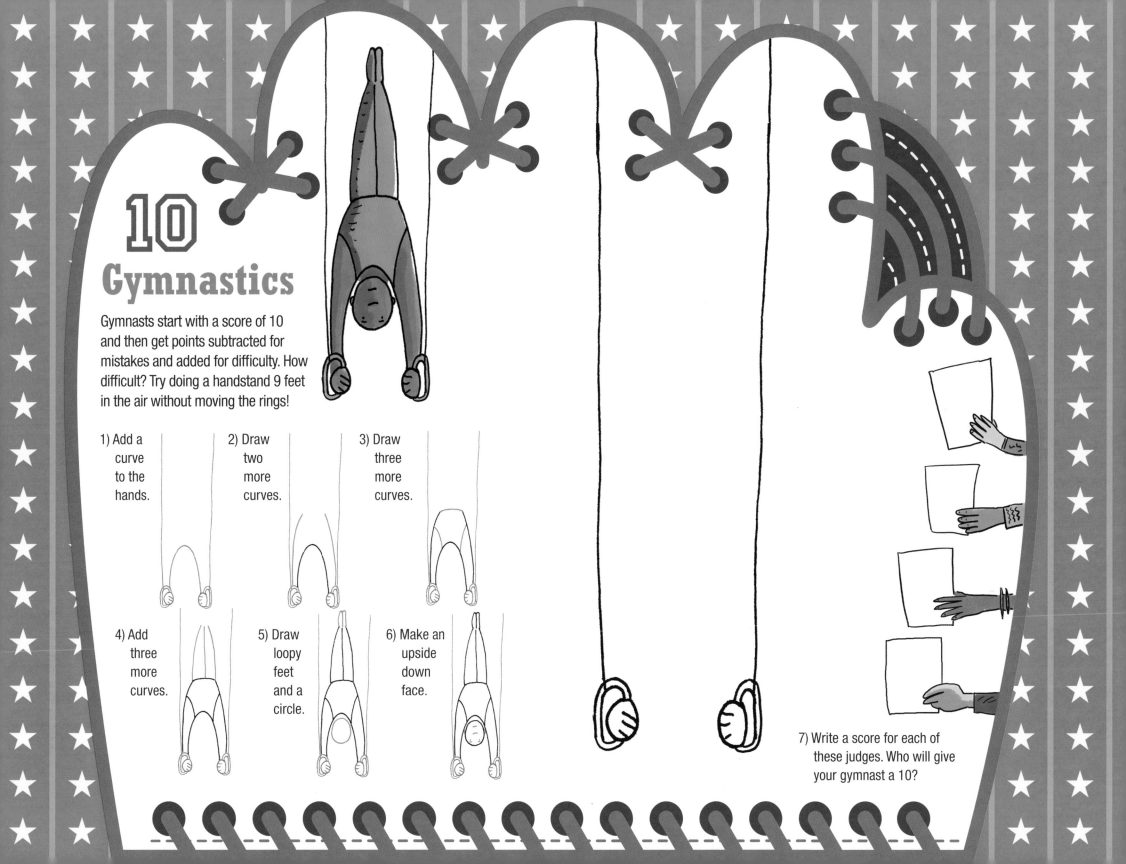

11 Football Goalposts

Two teams of 11 players each try to get a foot-long football across a 100-yard field to score a touchdown.

What's a centipede's favorite sport?

Feetball!

The 100-yard field is divided into ten 10-yard sections. Two 20-yard zones are at each end.

0 10 20 30 40 50 40 30 20 10 0

1) Draw an 11.

2) Connect at the bottom.

3) Attach a curve and a rectangle.

4) Add a football kicked for a field goal and a ref.

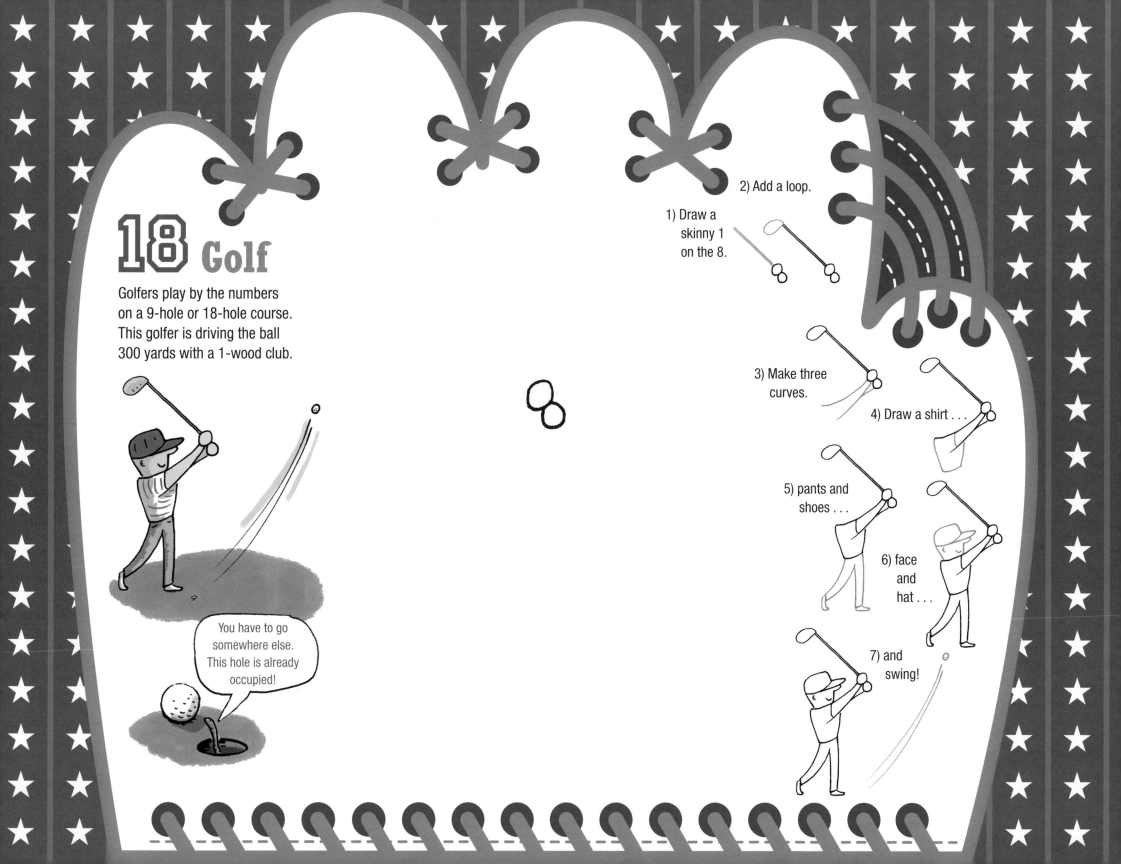

18 Golf

Golfers play by the numbers on a 9-hole or 18-hole course. This golfer is driving the ball 300 yards with a 1-wood club.

You have to go somewhere else. This hole is already occupied!

1) Draw a skinny 1 on the 8.

2) Add a loop.

3) Make three curves.

4) Draw a shirt . . .

5) pants and shoes . . .

6) face and hat . . .

7) and swing!

20
Pole Vault

It's simple. Take a long pole, run as fast as you can, stick the pole in the ground and catapult yourself 20 feet in the air! It's simple and almost impossible—Sergey Bubka is the only athlete to vault 20 feet.

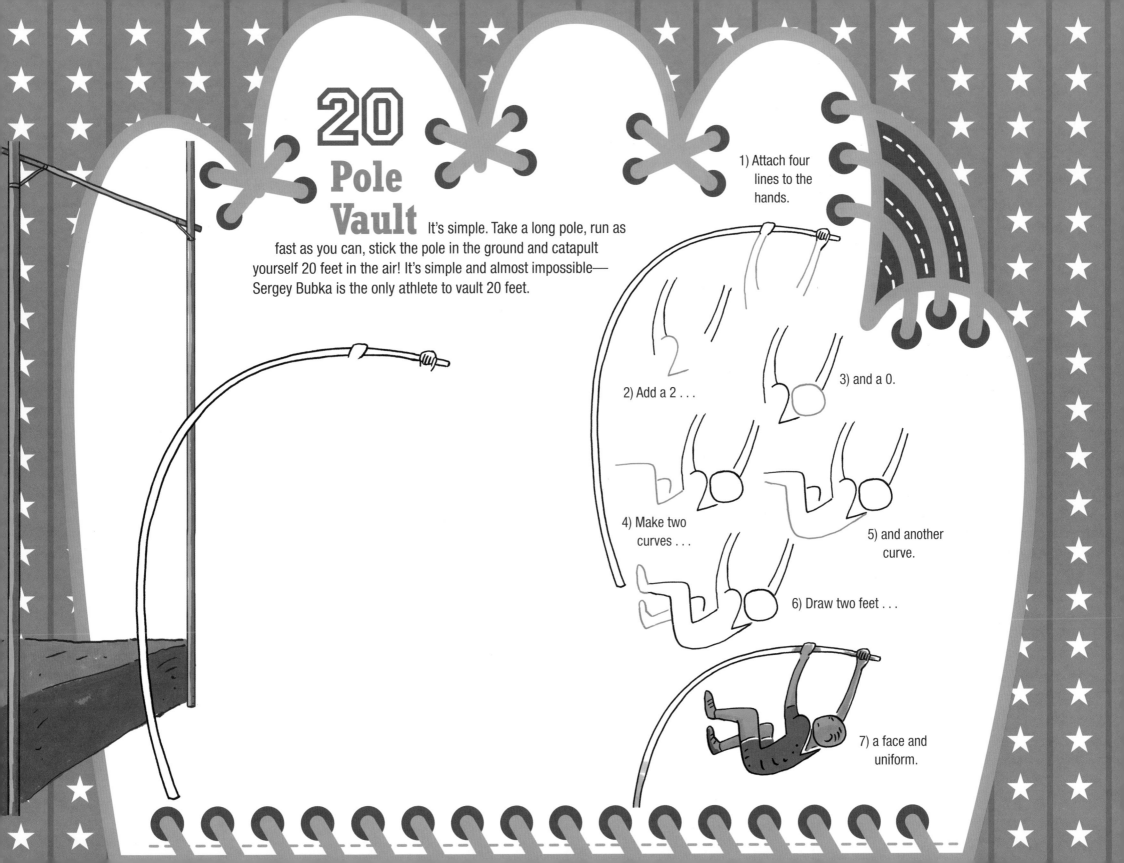

1) Attach four lines to the hands.

2) Add a 2 . . .

3) and a 0.

4) Make two curves . . .

5) and another curve.

6) Draw two feet . . .

7) a face and uniform.

100 Butterfly Swimming

1) Make an egg shape around the 100.

2) Draw goggles and a cap.

3) Attach four curves . . .

4) four more curves . . .

5) and loopy fingers.

6) Take a breath and make a splash!

\ O   O

Can a butterfly swim? No, but the best men and women swimmers can swim the butterfly stroke 100 meters in less than a minute!

360

Snowboarding

Spin all the way around in the air to do a 360. Or turn all the way upside down and right side up again for a 360 flip.

Why is it called a 360? Because a circle has 360 degrees. If you had a pie . . .

and you ate this piece, you ate 90 degrees of pie . . .

180 degrees of pie . . .

270 degrees of pie . . .

You ate a 360!

1) Start with a 360 circle.

2) Add a line and curve.

3) Make a squared U.

4) Draw two curves . . .

5) an arm and mitten . . .

6) a leg and a boot.

7) Make a board and make your move!

500
Car Race

Imagine driving in a circle 200 times at 185 miles per hour! The Indy 500 car race is 500 miles around a 2.5-mile track.

1) Connect the two zeroes with a line.

2) Add a 5 in a box.

3) Make a hook and a curve.

4) Draw two curves and a line on top . . .

5) a box, a U, two lines . . .

6) two wheels and a driver.

Flags tell drivers when to stop and when to go!

Green: Go!

Yellow: Be careful!

Red: Stop!

Black: You made a big mistake and are out of the race!

Checkered: Finish! If you pass this first, you're the winner!

Doodle and Drawing Fun for Everyone!

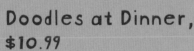

Doodles at Dinner, $10.99

An assortment of doodle placemats for doodling a variety of fun objects.

Fairy Doodles Placemats, $10.99

Each placemat offers a fairy-oriented drawing activity, light instructions, and interesting trivia about what's being drawn.

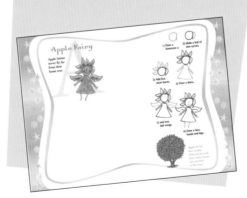

D is 4 Doodles, $12.99

Take some doodles on the road: includes a sturdy suface for drawing and perforated pages.

BLUE APPLE